CREDIT SCORE REPAIR

A step-by-step beginner's guide to learn how to repair your credit score

TABLE OF CONTENTS

- BY LAW 2
- CHAPTER 1 6
  - WHAT IS CREDIT SCORE? 6
  - CREDIT REPORTING AGENCIES 10
  - UNDERSTANDING CREDIT SCORING 12
  - CREDIT SCORES - HOW DO THEY WORK? 19
  - ARE THERE DIFFERENT KINDS OF CREDIT SCORES? 29
  - Is the number important? 31
  - How can I change my credit use to get a better score? 32
  - IS A CREDIT SCORE PART OF A CREDIT REPORT? 33
  - How do I get a credit score? 34
  - NEGATIVE ITEMS ON YOUR CREDIT REPORT 35
  - WHAT IS A GOOD CREDIT SCORE? 41
- CHAPTER 2 48
  - A BIGINNNER'S GUIDE TO CREDIT SCORE REPAIR 48
  - 10 CREDIT SCORE FACTS AND FICTIONS 53
  - ASSESS 66
  - DISPUTE 70
  - FOLLOW UP 78
  - MONITORING 82
- CHAPTER 3 84
  - HOW TO MAINTIAN YOUR CREDIT HEALTH OVER TIME 84
  - TRY REMOVING NEGATIVE ITEMS THAT AREN'T ERRORS 87
  - STICK TO A BUDGET 97
  - USE A SECURED CREDIT CARD RESPONSIBLY 101
- CHAPTER 4 105
  - HOW TO RECOGNIZE A CREDIT REPAIR SCAM 105
  - CAN ANY CREDIT REPAIR COMPANY BE TRUSTED? 109
  - AVOIDING CREDIT REPAIR SCAMS 111
- CONCLUSION 114

BY LAW:

- You're entitled to a free credit report if a company takes "adverse action" against you, like denying your application for credit, insurance, or employment. You have to ask for your report within 60 days of receiving notice of the action. The notice includes the name, address, and phone number of the consumer reporting company. You're also entitled to one free report a year if you're unemployed and plan to look for a job within 60 days; if you're on welfare; or if your report is inaccurate because of fraud, including identity theft.

- Each of the nationwide credit reporting companies — Equifax, Experian, and TransUnion — is required to provide you with a free copy of your credit report once every 12 months, if you ask for it. To order, visit annualcreditreport.com, call 1-877-322-8228, or use the form at the center of this booklet. You may order reports from each of the three credit reporting companies at the same time, or you can stagger your requests throughout the year.

- It doesn't cost anything to dispute mistakes or outdated items on your credit report. Both the credit reporting company and the information provider (the person, company, or organization that provides information about you to a credit reporting company) are responsible for correcting inaccurate or incomplete information in your report. To take advantage of all your rights, contact both the credit reporting company and the information provider.

Copyright 2018 by Jon Blake - All rights reserved.

This document is geared towards providing exact and reliable information in regards to the topic and issue covered. The publication is sold with the idea that the publisher is not required to render accounting, officially permitted, or otherwise, qualified services. If advice is necessary, legal or professional, a practiced individual in the profession should be ordered.

- From a Declaration of Principles which was accepted and approved equally by a Committee of the American Bar Association and a Committee of Publishers and Associations.

In no way is it legal to reproduce, duplicate, or transmit any part of this document in either electronic means or in printed format. Recording of this publication is strictly prohibited and any storage of this document is not allowed unless with written permission from the publisher. All rights reserved.

The information provided herein is stated to be truthful and consistent, in that any liability, in terms of inattention or otherwise, by any usage or abuse of any policies, processes, or directions contained within is the solitary and utter responsibility of the recipient reader. Under no circumstances will any legal responsibility or blame be held against the publisher for any reparation, damages, or monetary loss due to the information herein, either directly or indirectly.

Respective authors own all copyrights not held by the publisher.

The information herein is offered for informational purposes solely, and is universal as so. The presentation of the information is without contract or any type of guarantee assurance.

The trademarks that are used are without any consent, and the publication of the trademark is without permission or backing by the trademark owner. All trademarks and brands within this book are for clarifying purposes only and are the owned by the owners themselves, not affiliated with this document.

CHAPTER 1

WHAT IS CREDIT SCORE?

Basics

- A credit score is a numerical rating used by lenders in the loan approval decision process.
- Credit scoring uses statistical models to evaluate credit risk by comparing credit information about a consumer to the credit performance of others with similar credit reports.
- Credit bureaus keep track of everyone's credit history information – things like how many credit cards you have and how much you owe; whether you pay your bills on time; where you work and for how long.
- Credit scores may also be used to determine the interest rate you get on a loan. By using credit scores, lenders and

creditors treat each person objectively because the same standards apply to everyone.

- Credit scores do not include race, religion, national origin, gender or marital status as factors

A credit score is a number of 3 digits that lenders use as an indicator of your capacity to meet financial obligations such as mortgage payments, car payments, credit card bills, loan repayment, etc. It basically tells lenders how likely you are to pay your debts.

It is usually a number between 300 and 850. The higher the credit score, the less risky you are to lenders. And the less risky you are to lenders, the better interest rates you will get. Also, the higher your credit score is, the more chances you have in getting a loan. Sounds simple right?

A score of 750 or more will give you the best interest rates and the best chance of being approved for a loan. On the other hand, with a of 600 or less you will have a hard time finding a lender who is willing to give you a loan. And if you find it, you will have to pay a lot of money in interest just because of that low score.

Credit Risk :

Credit risk is the term within the credit industry to refer to the level of risk or likelihood of an individual borrower's future or potential default.

Credit Reports :

A credit report provides a history of your use of credit. Specifically, it's a file maintained by a credit reporting agency that contains information about a person, such as where the individual works and lives; information reported to the credit reporting agency by creditors regarding money borrowed and payments made; and public record information, such as whether the person has filed for bankruptcy.

Credit Score :

A credit score is a numerical value determined by a statistical model based upon past credit behaviors, which predicts the likelihood of future loan default.

CREDIT REPORTING AGENCIES

There are three major credit reporting agencies that will offer you the one free credit report you get each year. They are Experian, TransUnion, and Equifax. You can contact each of them directly in the following ways:

Equifax – Online, you can find them at www.equifax.com. You can also order your free credit report by mail. However, they only offer this option for free to residents in the states of Colorado, Georgia, Maine, Maryland, Massachusetts, New Jersey, and Vermont. All other states are required to pay a $10 fee. If you do want to do this by mail, send your request to Equifax Information Services, LLC; Disclosure Department; P.O. Box 740241; Atlanta, GA 30374. You can also call them at 1-800-685-1111.

TransUnion – Their web address is www.transunion.com. As with Equifax, you can also make your request via mail by getting a copy of their mail request form online and sending it to the address provided. You can also call them at 1-877-322-8228.

Experian – www.experian.com is where you can make a request for a credit report from this credit reporting agency. As with TransUnion, you will need to download a form from their website if you wish to request your credit report by mail. By phone you can call 888 397 3742.

UNDERSTANDING CREDIT SCORING

Basics

- Credit scores are used – along with your credit report and other information from your loan or credit application – to determine your eligibility for a loan.
- Credit scores speed up the loan approval process.
- Just as with your credit and credit behavior, credit scores change over time.
- Your credit score can impact your ability to get a credit card, purchase a home, borrow money, and whether or not you can get service from utility companies.

Loan :

Money you borrow from a financial institution with a written promise to pay it back later. With a loan, financial institutions will charge you fees and interest to borrow the money.

Interest Rate:

Interest rates are commonly thought of as the cost of borrowing money. The interest rate is expressed as a percentage. The amount of interest that is paid each year is determined by multiplying the amount of the loan by the percentage.

Lenders :

Lender is the term used for the person or entity that is providing credit or a loan to a borrower at specific terms and conditions. The term lender can generally be used interchangeably with the term creditor.

Creditors :

Creditor is the term used for the person or entity that is providing credit or a loan to a borrower at specific terms and conditions. The term creditor can generally be used interchangeably with the term lender.

Your credit score is one of the most critical factors in your financial life. It determines if you will be approved for a loan or line of credit. A credit score is a mathematically calculated number developed by the Fair Isaac Corporation (FICO) that lenders use to rate potential customers in determining the likelihood that a customer will pay their bills on time. A credit score or credit rating is determined by using five main criteria. Your payment history which accounts for 35% of your credit score, the amounts owed which accounts for 30% of your credit score, the length of your credit history which accounts for 15% of your credit score, new credit which accounts for 10% of your credit score, and the types of credit used which accounts for 10% of your credit score.

Payment history shows the history of how you paid your bills either on time or late but unfortunately does not show if your bills were paid before the due date.

Amounts owed shows the total amount of credit you have available. If your balance is near the credit limit this may lower your credit score. The length of history indicates how long you have had credit. If your credit history is 2 years or less could lower your credit score. New credit indicates how many times you have applied for new credit. If you open two many new accounts in a short period of time this may lower your credit score.

The types of credit used indicate the types of accounts you have such as revolving or installment accounts. Revolving accounts are usually credit cards and installment accounts are usually mortgages, auto loans, etc.

Having a good credit score can save you thousands of dollars in interest over the life of the loan or line of credit. A good credit score is generally in the range of 660-749 but may vary from lender to lender.

The three major credit bureaus Experian, Equifax and TransUnion use the FICO credit score model. Equifax uses the Beacon credit score, Experian uses the Fair Isaac or Plus score and TransUnion uses the Empirica score. Each credit bureau subscribes to the Fair Isaac's FICO model of scoring and then integrates their own version of a consumer's FICO score.

The Equifax Beacon score ranges from 340-820. The TransUnion Empirica score ranges from 150-934. The Fair Isaac or Plus score ranges from 330-830.

When applying for credit or a loan if all three credit scores are pulled, the middle score is generally the score used with the application, but according to the Fair Isaac Corporation 75% of mortgage loan applications use the Fair Isaac or Plus score.

Your credit score varies from each bureau because each agency collects their own data from various sources and may collect different data for the same account. Your score can vary anywhere from 5-40 points between the three credit bureaus. Your credit score changes due to updates to your credit file which changes based on account activity such as balance changes or additions to your credit file (i.e. new accounts or deletion of older negative accounts more than 7 or 10 years old). As a result, you may see a difference in your score from one month to the next.

The Following Criteria Are Not Concluded In Calculating Your Credit Score:

1. If rent or you own a home

2. Income

3. Length of time at your current job

4. Length of time at your current address

5. Whether you've been denied credit

CREDIT SCORES - HOW DO THEY WORK?

In today's current economy, its much harder to qualify for a loan. Now you need a very good credit score to qualify for most types of credit. So what's a good credit score rating? 850 is perfect credit and the highest credit score rating possible, though I've never personally seen anyone with an 850. A good credit score starts in the 670 range. Scores lower than 670 are not considered good credit.

How to Get a Good Credit Score:

There are 5 criteria that your credit is scored upon, and they're rather simple to follow.

1. Payment History Accounts For 35% Of Your Credit Score.

Do you pay your bills on time? If you do nothing else but make timely payments, you will have a good credit score in two years. Obviously, avoiding new collections, court actions, and most easily late pays will help your credit.

Past delinquency plays the largest role in hurting your credit score. One recent 30 day late payment will lower your credit score, most likely by 20 points! A couple of late payments, and your score will drop very far, very fast. 60 day lates hurt your score even more and 90 day lates are a real issue. It is important to know that the more recent the delinquency, the more negative the effect on your score.

One 30 day late last month will hurt more than even a 90 day late 4-5 years ago (5-10 points). Make sure to stay on top of your debt. Take caution to make timely payments and take care of accounts before they are late or go to collection. Do not overextend yourself in such a way that it hurts your chances of making timely payments. If you have old late pays that cannot be disputed off your credit report, know that time does heal old wounds and your score will increase given that no new delinquencies are reporting.

Pay before the Grace Period on your Credit Cards. Creditors charge additional fees for late payments. This is a very large profit center for a bank. Now, not only is there a due date, but there is also a due time. A bank may charge a $30-$35 fee for being 2 hours late on your payments! (make sure to look at the fine print of all agreements) Also, many banks have implemented under 20 day grace periods, shortened from 30 days, to increase overdue charges. Don't wait for the due date! Get your payments in fast or sign up for automatic debit payments online.

2. Amount Owed Accounts For 30% Of Your Credit Score.

The credit scoring model calculates credit balance against your high credit limit. This is calculated in percentages. It's important to keep your balances as low as possible.

If you have a card with a $5,000 credit limit, keeping your balance below $500 puts you in the 10% range of available credit. There are thresholds in debt ratio that will make your credit score jump higher. These thresholds are 70%, 50%, 30% and 10%. If you can't pay off your credit cards all the way, pay them down BELOW the next possible threshold. Calculate your credit limits in this way.

If you have a card with a $5,000 limit, multiply 5000 x.10 (or.30,.50,.70) You will want to pay your balance below these amounts. In this case - less than $500 (or $1500, $2500 or $3500).

Remember, the first thing to do is to check your credit report for credit limits. If your high limit is not reporting, the scoring model will use your balance as your credit limit. This means you're using 100% of your availability. Call your creditor and make sure they correct it. Distribution of debt is an easy way to make sure you maintain a strong score. Try to have a good spread of debt with lower balance to limit ratio. For example, its better to have $2,000 on five cards than it is to have $10,000 on one card with four others paid off.

If you're bumping up towards your credit limits, apply for more credit, or ask for an increase in credit from your existing accounts. This criteria is based on total availability, not size of availability. It doesn't matter if you borrow $500 or $50,000. It's how you handle it that matters. Distributing debt onto additional cards or credit lines can help you raise your score quickly.

3. Length Of Credit History Accounts For 15% Of Your Credit Score.

Length of credit history means how long you've had your credit accounts. If you've had an account for 15 years, it is stronger than a having a new account open for only two months. An important tip here is to never close your credit cards. Keep your old accounts open if they are in good standing, even if you don't use them and there's a zero balance. Remember though, you do need to use your credit lines at least every 6 months.

Accounts unused for 6 months become inactive and are ignored by the credit bureaus, unless there is a delinquent activity attached to that account. Keeping your credit lines open also aids in improving your credit availability, explained in the previous section.

If seeking to add credit, ask your card company to increase your credit limit. The best place to increase your credit lines, aside from getting a new card, is to extend your line on an old account with a good long history. Make sure they report the credit amount increase to the bureaus accurately.

One common factor of extremely good credit scores are long credit histories. Credit reports that have old accounts with a 15-

20 year history are likely to have much higher scores. It is, however, possible to add an old tradelines to your credit report.

4. Amount Of New Credit Accounts For 10% Of Your Credit Score.

New credit means brand new accounts recently open. You do have to start somewhere, but build slowly. If you have just applied for 10 credit cards, banks tend to assume the possibility that maybe you've lost your job and are in need of a back up plan. Try to start with one small line of credit and build from there. Make sure that you can handle the payments consistently, are never late, and keep your balances as low as possible, or completely paid off.

5. Type Of Credit Used Accounts For 10% Of Your Credit Score.

The credit scoring model likes to see that you have a variety of types of credit in your file. The very best placement of credit is to have a loan on a home, a car payment and a few credit cards. This credit is spread across different types of lenders and type of credit extended to you. There are a few types of credit to stay away from. Payday loans are very bad places to have credit with and your scores take a hit for having these types of high risk loans. Other very bad types of credit are the offers that allow you to have no payments for a year. These are dangerous, because the terms of the agreement may include that if you do not pay the loan off in a year, on day 366 you will owe the entire years worth of payments at typically 20% interest. This is a disaster waiting to happen. People who repeatedly go for these offers, are people who get into credit trouble. You should not have that kind of credit on your credit report.

"Knowledge is power" and the most important step to applying for a loan is to understand your credit report, your credit scores and how credit scoring works. It is highly recommended that every person checks their credit report at least once per year to help protect themselves from inaccurate information and from identity theft. A new law was recently passed that permits a borrower to have access to their credit report one time each year for no charge to allow them the opportunity to review their credit history and verify the accuracy of all items listed. You are permitted to obtain a credit report from each of the three credit repositories, TransUnion, Equifax, and Experian. You can obtain your free report by logging into the annual credit report and following the directions. When you obtain your free report it will not contain your credit score, but you can pay a small fee if you would like to find out what your score is when you are ordering your free report. It is also highly recommended that you pull a report from each repository individually as opposed to all of them together so that you can dispute any erroneous information to each bureau separately. If you report a problem to only one of the bureaus it will not be fixed among all three of the bureaus. Remember the bureaus are separate of each other and have no communication amongst each other either. Some creditors report to only 1 bureau, some report to 2 bureaus, some report to all three bureaus and some don't report to any. This is why you must make sure that you check all three credit repositories when you are utilizing your free annual credit report. In conclusion, your credit is very important and understanding the basics of how your credit scores are obtained is equally as important.

ARE THERE DIFFERENT KINDS OF CREDIT SCORES?

There are many different credit score models produced by a number of different companies. Experian's Decision Analytics business, separate from its credit reporting business, develops credit scores for lenders and other companies. There are other companies that specialize in creating credit scores as well. Additionally, some businesses, including lenders and insurance companies, develop their own credit scores based on their experience with customers.

Generic credit scores indicate general financial risk and may be used by many different companies. Custom scores are developed to predict risk for specific types of lending or for individual businesses. For example, one credit score model may evaluate the repayment risk for retail debt. Another model may be specifically for auto loan repayment. There even are credit scores used to help predict bankruptcy risk or the likelihood a person will make an insurance claim. Usually, though, if one type of credit score indicates a person is low risk, other scores also will predict low risk because the same credit history information is used to make the calculations.

Is the number important?

The answer, of course, is "yes." The score is important, but the number is meaningful only in the context of that particular score range and that particular business transaction.

Each business selects the scoring service it will use based on its particular needs and risk tolerance. Businesses establish their own policies for deciding if a particular score will result in approving or declining an application or, in some cases, if different prices or fees will apply based on the risk the score represents.

Outside of a specific transaction, though, a credit score is just a random number. Without additional information to explain what it means, the score is useless as a tool to improve your creditworthiness. With a credit report to put it in context, any score is a valuable educational tool.

How can I change my credit use to get a better score?

A credit score represents the information in your credit report. In order to improve your credit scores, you must address the information from your credit report that most affected the scores. That information is identified by risk factor statements, which are generated along with the score at the time it is calculated. The statements often are included in a declination letter sent by the lender when your application is declined. Addressing the factors should improve your creditworthiness over time and consequently result in better credit scores. For instance, paying a past-due debt generally will not immediately result in a huge improvement. However, keeping the payments current after paying the past-due debt will demonstrate good credit management, resulting in better credit scores over time.

IS A CREDIT SCORE PART OF A CREDIT REPORT?

A credit score is not part of a credit report. Credit reporting companies often are erroneously referred to as "credit rating agencies." In fact, neither credit reports nor credit reporting companies "rate" your credit. Credit scoring is a separate process from credit reporting.

How do I get a credit score?

Credit score reports are available for a fee from a number of sources, including Experian. Any score you receive through a consumer score disclosure service will explain what that number means in terms of general credit risk and will describe the factors from your credit report that most influenced the score.

NEGATIVE ITEMS ON YOUR CREDIT REPORT

The Fair Credit Reporting Act (FCRA) limits the length of time a credit bureau can report negative items on your credit report while positive and neutral items are usually reported indefinitely. Plus, the amount of damage each negative item causes on your score fades little by little over time. That means your bad credit can't last forever as long as you start implementing some positive behaviors.

Negative items can successfully be removed from your report before the usual time limit, although it's not always possible depending on your situation. You might also prefer spending your time getting newer negative items removed since older ones drop off sooner.

Here's a look at each type of negative item you may find on your credit report, and how long you can expect them to stay there if you can't or don't try to get them removed.

Charge Offs – A charge-off occurs when a creditor decides a debt is not collectible. Rather than carry it on their books as an overdue or past due debt, they can instead eliminate it from their reportable past due accounts.

By charging off the debt, the company's accounts receivable report improves; however, that doesn't mean the debt has disappeared. In most cases, the debt is sold to a "debt buyer" who pays pennies on the dollar for the face value of the debt.

By purchasing the debt, the debt buyer can now attempt to collect the amount owed (plus court fees, interest, late charges, and more) by contacting the debtor and taking them to court for the full value plus any applicable fees.

If you have a charge off on your credit report, it can stay there for up to seven years plus 180 days from the original date of delinquency.

Collections – Collections are complicated because paying them off may actually end up hurting your credit score by resetting the start date from when it was reported. Before taking action on collections, read on to find out how to navigate these murky waters.

Like charge offs, collection accounts may be reported for up to seven years from the date you first fell behind with the original creditor.

Late Payments – Even if you eventually catch up on what you owe, any payment that is more than 30 days late can appear on your credit report. However, some creditors don't report the past due payment until a second payment is owed because they don't want to upset good customers who simply forgot to the deadline and made it up the following month. Credit reporting rules do require that after a second payment is missed, all past due payments must be reported.

Late payments or delinquent accounts may be reported for up to seven years after the date of the last scheduled payment.

Bankruptcies – Bankruptcies may be reported for no more than ten years from the date you initially filed. If your case was dismissed, the ten years starts from the date of dismissal. The amount of time also depends on the type of bankruptcy you filed. Chapter 13 bankruptcies stay on for only seven years, while Chapter 7 bankruptcies remain on your credit report for the full ten years.

Foreclosures – Foreclosures may also be reported for up to seven years. Luckily, you don't have to wait that long to buy a new house once you regain your financial footing. You could qualify for a mortgage as soon as two years, though sometimes longer depending on the type of loan.

Judgments – Judgments may be reported for up to seven years from the date the lawsuit was filed or until the governing statute of limitations has expired, whichever is longer. Most statutes of limitation are shorter than seven years, so that is the likely maximum time a judgment or lawsuit will show up on your credit report. To be sure, check your specific state laws for details.

Repossessions – Repossessions may be reported for up to seven years as well. It's worth noting that regardless of whether it's listed on your credit report, you are still financially responsible for any remaining debt after the property (such as a car) has been repossessed.

Tax Liens – Under federal law, unpaid tax liens may be reported on your credit reports indefinitely. However, the credit bureaus could remove them after a decade or so. Paid tax liens may be reported from the date of payment for up to seven years.

WHAT IS A GOOD CREDIT SCORE?

Basics

- The most commonly used credit score is known as a FICO® score.

- FICO scores are ranked on a scale of approximately 300-900 points.

  Here's how credit scores might be grouped:

  - 720-850 = Excellent
  - 680-719 = Good
  - 640-679 = Fair
  - 350-639 = Poor
  - <349 = No Credit

- Generally, the higher the score, the lower the predicted risk to the lender.

- You can obtain a copy of your credit score online for a small fee at www.myfico.com

- When applying for a loan, ask your lender or creditor to explain what your credit score means in relation to the final credit decision.

- Never assume that your score is good or impaired until it has been fully explained to you by a credit industry professional.

There are several items to think about when one is pondering what is a good credit score. One way of estimating the ability of a borrower to pay back a loan is to look at that individual's credit score.

The scores can be high or low or in the middle. If a score is high, then it is assumed that a person would be able to obtain valuable credit and can easily pay back funds loaned to them. If a score is low, the perception is the opposite. A low score will make lenders cautious and it will not be easy for one to have monies extended to them. In a lender's eyes, various scores may mean different things, depending on the type of scoring system that particular creditor uses. This valuable credit score one obtains is helpful to those deciding whether or not to loan funds. Those entities extending credit can figure out the amount of money to offer an individual and with what interest rate as well.

Credit scores are composed of a varying degree of numbers, anywhere from 300-850. A score is made up of a range of pertinent factors. A look at the payment history information consists of thirty-five percent of the score. Observing the amount a person owes is thirty percent. The credit history longevity is fifteen percent of the score. New spending information composes ten percent. Consideration of the various kinds of credit used is the remaining ten percent of the score number.

One free annual credit report can be obtained from each of the credit companies for a total count of three reports a year.

It is very important to digest the contents that are on one's report with a fine tooth comb. Information that is not accurate and correct can sometimes be found. Sometimes errors in late payment content, payment histories and amounts of monies owed can be seen. A person can be certain in reviewing the report that there is no identity theft as well.

Entities extending credit will be careful in looking closely at numbers on an individual's credit scores. For the most part, lenders feel that a score of 700 or above is thought to be very good to excellent. One would value keeping their scores high due to the many advantages of toning a high credit number. Credit extensions with low interest rate offers would be secured by the high scoring report owners. Also, fast credit approval processes can be received by those with that excellent high score!

In the list below, one can see the value in looking through the eyes of a credit lender to take in the information as they perceive it: Excellent credit is a score of 760 or above. Very good credit is a notch below with that 700 to 759 score. A good score falls in the range of 680-699. An okay score is 620-679. A fair or so-so number is summed up in the 580-619 bracket. If a score lies in the 300-579 area, the score is considered poor.

It is valuable to the one wanting credit to critique their report approximately six to twelve months before applying for a big loan. In checking the report and seeing the score, one can look for any errors and make sure details are listed correctly.

This time frame allows a credit seeker the opportunity to begin a process of making corrections where needed if errors were found. If errors still show on the report at the time of applying for a large loan, one must tell the lender of these mistakes.

There is the possibility to improve one's credit score. This can be done in seeing that monies owed are regularly paid, reducing outstanding account balances.

Since timeliness of payments is noted on every report, it is vital to make payments on time. It would be in the borrower's best interest to not take on new debt.

There Are A Few Pointers To Keep In Mind In Seeking To Receive A Good Credit Score:

Credit advisors are available to help in a crisis financial position where payments cannot be made. Also, the creditors themselves are most likely willing to help in any way they can, including lowering and spreading out payments. It would be advantageous to talk with creditors and credit advisors. Credit card balances must not be allowed to sky-rocket. Maintaining low balances is the key.

Some individuals may think it wise to close old accounts to try to hide any late payments shown on these accounts. It is not realistic to think that closed accounts will improve one's credit score. Even if an account is closed, the late payment history will continue to show on the credit report.

Those lending money desire to see a credit history with active borrowing that goes back several years or more.

Keen insights and careful thought will go along way to achieve what is a good credit score range. Achieving this will go along way in your personal financial life.

CHAPTER 2

A BIGINNNER'S GUIDE TO CREDIT SCORE REPAIR

Bad credit score is just what it sounds like; bad!

It is not a desirable thing to have your unpaid bills pile up as it will subsequently take its toll on your happiness and hence the quality of your life.

Your FICO score or credit score follows you like a shadow throughout your life. Whatever you do that involves paying bills with your credit card or getting loans reflects on your credit score either positively or negatively.

Borrowing money to settle most outstanding bills often incur some rates, which are always higher for customers with a low or bad credit score. A credit score is a number between 300 and 850 and a bad credit score ranges between 300 to 629 points.

If you are a beginner to credit card usage and happen to find yourself in the mess of bad credit, here are some guidelines that will help you manage and successfully repair your credit score.

1. Pay Attention To Your Payment History :

Your payment history makes up the largest proportion and gathers the most significant number of points on your credit score. The quickest way to destroy your credit score is to have reduced points on payment history.

When you obtain loans, you need to pay back as at when due and in full. Failure to do so will take points from your payment history, which has the largest impact on your credit score.

2. Check Your Credit Statement Thoroughly :

Your creditors may have made one or two errors in your credit report which could be affecting your score negatively. When you do a thorough check and find errors, dispute them. We are not saying these credit report errors are common, but they do happen sometimes.

Once you get your report and discover a mistake, have a copy that highlights the error and of course any other copy of your proof, like bank account details. Credit score calculation firms will do nothing without proof!

You can write the company through a letter, certified mail or online. Ensure you keep a copy for yourself and await your reply after thirty days.

Do Not Spend More Than You Can Afford :

After a thorough check and cleanup have been done on your credit report, ensure that you do not spend more than you can afford each month.

You can find out how much you make in a year by quickly reviewing your tax returns for the previous 2 or more years.

Next is to ascertain your regular monthly expenses and your monthly spending habits. Subtract your regular monthly expenses from your monthly income and try not to live above the difference monthly, by cutting down on every other expense.

Do Not Get A New Credit Account :

If your current credit score is messed up, do not fall for the seductive option of getting a new credit card no matter how sweet a deal it sounds. Creating a new account gives rise to 'inquiry' from credit companies.

If you have too many accounts opened within the space of two years, your already bad credit score will only continue to decline.

10 CREDIT SCORE FACTS AND FICTIONS

When it comes to credit, knowledge is very essential . Here are the real facts behind 10 common credit score fictions:

1. Fiction: The More Money You Make, The Better Your Credit Score Will Fare.

Fact: Your income has nothing to do with your credit score. It's not reported to the credit bureaus or listed on your credit report.

2. Fiction: Once You've Paid A Past-Due Debt, It Will Drop Off Of Your Credit Report.

Fact: Late payments and other negative information remain on your credit report for seven years from the date of the initial late payment. Bankruptcies typically stick around for 10 years from the bankruptcy filing date. While that black mark may continue to soil your report, however, its effect on your score will lessen over time.

3. Fiction: Credit Bureaus And Those Reporting To Them Never Make Mistakes.

Fact: Nearly eight in 10 credit reports contain a serious error or some sort of mistake, according to a survey by the U.S. Public Interest Research Groups. Because many errors can negatively impact your score, it's important to check your report regularly and dispute any inaccuracies you find.

4. Fiction: Practicing A Cash-Only Policy Will Help Your Credit Score.

Fact: Having good credit is a function of having credit available to you and using it responsibly. If you don't have or use credit, you may have no credit history at all and if you do, your score won't be as good as someone who consistently demonstrates responsible use of credit over time.

5. Fiction: All Credit Reports And Scores Are The Same.

Fact: You have three main credit reports - one from Experian, Equifax and Transunion - plus a variety of credit scores. The information listed on each of your reports may vary, and your scores - even if based on a single report - may also vary. No one report or score is better than the others. They all seek to document your credit history and assess your default risk.

6. Fiction: How Responsibly You Manage Your Checking, Savings And Investment Accounts Will Impact Your Credit Score.

Fact: Like income, your checking, savings and investment account activity is not reported to the credit bureaus and does not affect your score.

7. Fiction: Closing Credit Card Accounts Will Help Your Credit Score.

Fact: When you close a credit card account, you may be affecting your "credit utilization," which is simply how much credit you use (balances) compared to how much is available to you (limits) - the lower, the better. Closing a card lowers the amount of credit that's available to you, which may increase your utilization percentage if you maintain balances on any of your other cards. A higher credit utilization may negatively impact your score.

8. Fiction: Pulling Your Own Credit Report Will Lower Your Credit Score.

Fact: When you pull your credit report for your own educational purposes, it's considered a "soft inquiry" and will not affect your credit score. On the other hand, when a creditor or lender pulls your report for the purpose of extending you credit or a loan, it's a "hard inquiry" and may negatively impact your score.

9. Fiction: If A Bill Or Debt Isn't Generally Reported To The Credit Bureaus, Missing A Payment Won't Affect Your Credit Score.

Fact: Any time you pay a bill late or don't pay at all, that activity can be reported to the credit bureaus.

Different companies have different policies about reporting late payments or negative information, but never assume that just because you've never seen a particular bill listed on your credit report that it can't negatively impact your credit score if you don't pay it.

10. Fiction: Disputing Accurate Information Will Remove It From Your Credit Report.

Fact: You can only dispute information on your credit report that is inaccurate. When you dispute information on your report, the credit bureau has 30 days to investigate. If it finds the dispute to be valid, it will remove the inaccurate information. If, however, the dispute claim is found to be false, that information will not be removed from your report.

Credit Repair Companies often make big promises. You might have received offers that sounded a Bit like this:

- We can erase your bad credit – 100% guaranteed
- Create a new credit identity – legally
- We can remove bankruptcies, judgments and liens forever!

If you have a bad credit score, these companies can be tempting. How nice would it be if you could just pay someone to make your bad credit disappear forever? Unfortunately, you can not legally hide from debt that is yours.

Credit Repair Companies Tend To Use One Of The Following Tactics:

Break the law: These companies will encourage you to create new Social Security Number or dispute debt that you know is yours, which is illegal. As the Federal Trade Commission makes clear, "no one can legally remove accurate and timely negative information from a credit report." Charge you a fee to do things you can do for yourself at little or no cost: These companies will not break the law. But they will charge you money to manage the process of removing inaccurate or incorrect information from your credit report.

You might decide that you want to pay someone to handle the process for you. But the purpose of this brief eBook is to help you do, for free, everything a credit repair company would do for a fee.

If you feel overwhelmed by the steps outlined in this eBook, you can consider paying someone to help you. Just make sure that the company you use is not a scam. Here are some of the biggest warning signs that a credit repair company is a scam:

- The company wants you to pay before it provides a service. Under federal law, credit repair companies can't require you to pay until they've completed the service they have promised.
- The company recommends that you don't contact any of the credit reporting agencies directly.
- The company tells you that it can get rid of negative credit information in your credit report, even if that information is accurate. No one can do this.
- The company suggest you try to invent a "new" credit identity – and then, a new credit report – by applying for an Employer Identification Number to use instead of your Social Security Number. This is a federal crime, and you would be liable!
- The company advises you to dispute all of the information in your credit report, regardless of its accuracy or timeliness.

If you have just signed up for these services, you have the right to cancel your contract with any credit repair organization for any reason within three business days.

Before we start, I just wanted to remind you that bad items on your credit report are not a life sentence. All negative information will eventually be removed from your credit report and the older an item the less impact they are going to have on your FICO score. For example, a collection item that is 5 years old will hurt much less than a collections item that is 5 months old. Here is how long it takes for items to leave your credit report

- Late payments: 7 years
- Bankruptcies: 7 years for completed Chapter 13 bankruptcies and 10 years for Chapter 7 bankruptcies
- Foreclosures: 7 years
- Collections: Generally, about 7 years, depending upon the age of the debt being collected Public record: Generally,

about 7 years, although unpaid tax liens can remain indefinitely. (always pay the tax man first!)

The best way to improve your score is to have good behavior reported every single month. Even if you have a terrible credit score, take out a secured credit card and use it monthly.

Charge no more than 10% of the available credit limit. (If your limit is $1,000 make sure your balance is never greater than $100). Pay the balance in full and on time every month. Your credit score will start to improve as your negative information ages and your credit report becomes increasingly filled with positive, good information.

We wish we could promise a miracle. But if you have bad credit because you missed payments or defaulted on other loans, there is no miracle other than time and discipline. If your credit score is suffering because of inaccuracies or abuse, we can help you get it fixed quickly.

Checklist for Credit Repair

1. ASSESS: Find out what is on your credit report from all 3 credit reporting agencies – for free
2. DISPUTE: Dispute incorrect information (You can do this online, and you can do with a letter. We provide sample letters that you can use.)
3. FOLLOW UP: Make sure you follow up and get that incorrect information removed.
4. MONITOR: Set up monitoring to ensure that you are notified as soon as the incorrect information is removed. Putting in place monitoring

will also alert you quickly if someone tries to open new accounts in your name.

We will now have a chapter dedicated to each step. We will explain in detail how to Assess, Dispute, Follow Up and Monitor.

ASSESS

Everyone is entitled to one free credit report from each credit reporting agency every year. It is important to get a full report from the credit reporting agency, and not just your credit score. Many sites and credit cards offer access to a free score. Seeing your score each month is a great perk, but you need a detailed credit report in order to do the assessment properly.

In this chapter, We Will Walk Through The Following Steps:

- Download a free copy of all three credit reports
- Review the credit report to find errors
- Prepare a list of items that you might need to dispute

1. Download a Free Copy of all 3 Credit Reports

There is only one official website where you can get your official credit reports from all three agencies for free: www.AnnualCreditReport.com.

Go to the homepage (pictured below) and click on "Request yours now!" to start the process. You can then download your report from all three reporting agencies.

Once you have downloaded your credit report with one of the credit reporting agencies, make sure you click "Get Your Next Report or Finish" on the top right of the screen to get your report from the next credit reporting agency.

With some reporting agencies (like Equifax), you might be asked security information. For example, you could be asked the name of your mortgage company, the amount of your monthly payment, or other personal information. Once you are authenticated, you will have the opportunity to download your credit report.

2. Review the Credit Report

Review your credit report in detail. When you review your credit report, you will want to make a list. On that list, you will write down anything that you think is incorrect. Here is what to look for:

- Do you recognize all of the accounts on your credit report? Write down any account that you do not think is yours.
- Do you recognize all of the inquiries on your credit report? (An inquiry is a record of any new credit that you apply for. If someone steals
- your identity and tries to apply for new credit in your name, an unrecognizable credit inquiry is usually the first sign of a problem)
- Review each account, and make sure that:

The account balance and payment history looks right. (For example, you might have an old credit card that you haven't used in years. But when you look online, you see a balance because could have stolen the account information).

The payment history is correct. You should be able to see 7 years of history. If you see missed payments that shouldn't have been there, write it down. Your credit score is negatively impacted when you are 30 days or more past due.

DISPUTE

If there is incorrect information on your credit report, you will need to take action.

The incorrect information could be on your credit report because:

- Someone stole your identity and opened new accounts in your name.
- Someone stole one of your existing accounts (for example, a bartender skims a card at the bar) and started using it.
- The bank made an error and reported a delinquency or default when it really didn't happen
- A collection agency made an error and reported a collection item on debt that was never yours.

If you have incorrect information on your credit report, you will need to dispute that information to the credit bureaus and the reporting organization (bank, collection agency, etc.). If your identity has been stolen, you will need to take some additional steps.

Was your identity stolen? When someone steals your identity, they have the ability to open new accounts in your name. And you often don't know that your identity has been stolen until you look at your credit report.

Imagine the following simple example: Someone (the criminal) manages to steal your Social Security Number. The criminal then applies for new credit cards in your name, but at a different address and phone number. The criminal uses that credit card but never pays. You never know about it because you are never called and no letter is ever sent to your home.

Here are some other symptoms of identity theft:

- You don't get your bills or other mail. Someone has managed to login to your accounts, change the mailing address, and start receiving everything at their address instead of yours.
- Debt collectors call you about debts that aren't yours
- Medical providers bill you for services you didn't use
- Your health plan rejects your legitimate medical claims because the records show you've reached your benefits limit
- The IRS notifies you that more than 1 tax return was filed in your name, or that you have income from an employer you don't work for
- You get notice that your information was compromised by a data breach at a company where you do business or have an account
- You are arrested for a crime someone else allegedly committed in your name

Warning: a very common form of identity theft happens within families. A brother, sister, cousin or uncle steals your Social Security Number and uses it to apply for credit. You might be very saddened, or angry about it. But you will not be alone. If you determine that your ID has been stolen, you need to take some additional important steps.

Visit www.identitytheft.gov to report identity theft and get a recovery plan. This is an excellent, free website created by the Federal Trade Commission (of the United States Government). You will be able to report your identity theft online. You will then get an action plan and will even have access to real people who can help you resolve your problem.

As an identity theft victim, you will be urged to do things like: Place a fraud alert on your account with the credit reporting agencies.

You can do that by calling: Equifax: 1-800-525-6285 Experian: 1-888-397-3742. TransUnion: 1-800-680-7289 Consider placing a credit freeze on your credit reports. A freeze blocks potential creditors from getting access to your credit report, making it less likely an identity thief can open new accounts in your name. Create an Identity Theft Report, which requires submitting a complaint about the theft to FTC and filing a police report. Once you go through all of these steps, you will then need to dispute errors with credit reporting companies. We will explain that process now.

How to Dispute Incorrect Information We recommend that you dispute information both online and in writing. You will need to dispute the incorrect information to: Every credit reporting agency (TransUnion, Experian and Equifax) that has the incorrect information Every creditor or other information provider (like a collection agency) that the information is incorrect. That should be done in writing.

Credit Reporting Agencies: Here is a sample letter, created by the FTC, that can help you dispute your credit information: [Your Name] [Your Address] [Your City, State, Zip Code] [Date] Complaint Department [Company Name] [Street Address] [City, State, Zip Code] Dear Sir or Madam: I am writing to dispute the following information in my file. I have circled the items I dispute on the attached copy of the report I received. This item [identify item(s) disputed by name of source, such as creditors or tax court, and identify type of item, such as credit account, judgment, etc.] is [inaccurate or incomplete] because [describe what is inaccurate or incomplete and why]. I am requesting that the item be removed [or request another specific change] to correct the information. Enclosed are copies of [use this sentence if applicable and describe any enclosed documentation, such as payment records and court documents] supporting my position.

Please reinvestigate this [these]matter[s] and [delete or correct] the disputed item[s] as soon as possible. Sincerely, Your name Enclosures: [List what you are enclosing.] **** It is very important that you:

Provide detailed information regarding your dispute.

Provide copies (not originals) of the supporting evidence. In addition to sending a letter, you can also dispute online. We recommend that you do both.

Below is a sample letter, created by the Consumer Financial Protection Bureau, that you can send to a collection agency. The purpose of this letter is to make it clear that you do not owe this debt. **** [Your name] [Your return address] [Date] [Debt collector name] [Debt collector address] Re: [Account number for the debt, if you have it] Dear [Debt collector name], I am responding to your contact about collecting a debt. You contacted me by [phone/mail], on [date] and identified the debt as [any information they gave you about the debt]. I do not have any responsibility for the debt you're trying to collect. If you have good reason to believe that I am responsible for this debt, mail me the documents that make you believe that. Stop all other communication with me and with this address, and record that I dispute having any obligation for this debt. If you stop your collection of this debt, and forward or return it to another company, please indicate to them that it is disputed. If you report it to a credit bureau (or have already done so), also report that the debt is disputed.

FOLLOW UP

Once you register your dispute with the credit reporting agencies, they must investigate the item in question – usually within 30 days – unless they consider your dispute frivolous. They also must forward all the relevant data you provide about the inaccuracy to the organization that provided the information. After the information provider receives notice of a dispute from the credit reporting company, it must investigate, review the relevant information, and report the results back to the credit reporting company. If the information provider finds the disputed information is inaccurate, it must notify all three nationwide credit reporting companies so they can correct the information in your file.

When the investigation is complete, the credit reporting company must give you the results in writing and a free copy of your report if the dispute results in a change. This free report does not count as your annual free report. If an item is changed or deleted, the credit reporting company cannot put the disputed information back in your file unless the information provider verifies that it is accurate and complete. The credit reporting company also must send you written notice that includes the name, address, and phone number of the information provider.

If you ask, the credit reporting company must send notices of any corrections to anyone who received your report in the past six months.

You can have a corrected copy of your report sent to anyone who received a copy during the past two years for employment purposes.

If an investigation doesn't resolve your dispute with the credit reporting company, you can ask that a statement of the dispute be included in your file and in future reports. You also can ask the credit reporting company to provide your statement to anyone who received a copy of your report in the recent past. You can expect to pay a fee for this service. And, unfortunately, a dispute on your credit report is not very helpful for improving your credit score.

Do I Have Any Other Options?

If you are unhappy with the way your case was investigated by the credit reporting agencies, you do not have to give up. Instead, you can complain to the Consumer Financial Protection Bureau (also known as the CFPB) on their website (www.consumerfinance.gov). All of your written correspondence with the credit reporting agencies, banks, credit unions and collection agencies becomes very important when you create your complaint. When you complain to the CFPB, you can should provide copies of all of your correspondence to prove your case. The CFPB will reach out to the credit reporting agencies on your behalf and try to help get your situation resolved. At MagnifyMoney, we have worked with many people who have had good outcomes working with the CFPB.

MONITORING

You should come up with a strategy to monitor your credit report on an on-going basis.

You don't have to pay for good credit monitoring services. You can do all of this for free. The best, free way to monitor your credit is with CreditKarma. Visit www.creditkarma.com and you will have 2 of the 3 credit reports monitored on a regular basis. You will be able to get alerts whenever a new account is opened in your name. There are services out there that charge a monthly fee. Your fee would add the following services:

- Monitor all three credit bureaus daily
- Resolution assistance in case your identity is stolen

If you have been a previous victim of identity theft, you might want to pay for three-bureau monitoring, to reduce your risk. To see a ranking of the best paid solutions, you can visit MagnifyMoney.

Credit monitoring is a great service. As soon as you detect suspicious activity, you can take action. The sooner you work to deal with issues in your credit report, the less damage that can be done.

CHAPTER 3

HOW TO MAINTIAN YOUR CREDIT HEALTH OVER TIME

10 Tips For Managing Your Credit Report To Maintain Your Scores

1. Establish a credit report: Creditors need financial references, and that is what your credit report provides. The report's content is used to calculate your credit scores.

2. Always pay on time as agreed: Late payments will negatively impact your ability to get credit and are the first signs of impending credit problems.

3. Have a mix of credit, but obtain and use a credit card: You decide how to use the card and repay the balance, which tells more about how you make credit decisions than other types of loans, such as auto loans or mortgages.

4. Use caution when deciding to close accounts: Closing accounts reduces your available credit. That can increase your total balance-to-limit ratio, which is a sign of risk and can negatively impact credit scores.

5. Apply for credit judiciously: Recent inquiries indicate you may have taken on new debt that isn't yet shown as an account on your credit report. Many inquiries in a short time might suggest you are trying to take on large amounts of debt. Both issues signify risk.

6. Time is the key: It takes some time for your credit report to be updated, so balances can't be reduced overnight. Additionally, credit scores not only look at whether your bills are paid, but also at how long they have been current and how far in the past negative information appears. It takes time for scores to improve after you have taken control of your credit.

7. Demonstrate stability: Lenders may look beyond your financial transactions and ask how long you have had your job, how long you have lived in the same location and whether you have built other assets over time.

8. Have a plan: Know how you are going to repay the debt when you use your credit card or get a loan, and stick to that plan.

9. Put credit to work for you: Use credit as a tool to take advantage of low interest rates, convenient shopping, rewards programs and financial management. When you are in control, credit works for you.

10. Share your knowledge: Share what you've learned about credit with your friends and family so that they can avoid pitfalls and mistakes you might have made.

TRY REMOVING NEGATIVE ITEMS THAT AREN'T ERRORS

On the other hand, let's say you've made some mistakes. You couldn't afford to pay your credit card bill. Your student loan payments are sometimes late. Of course, the ultimate solution is to improve your financial habits; that much is obvious. In the meantime, though, you still have options for dealing with the negative items on your report.

For late payments, you can draft a "goodwill letter," which is sometimes referred to as a "goodwill adjustment." If you generally have a good history with a creditor, they're often willing to forgive a late payment here and there and update your credit report accordingly. You'll want to contact the creditor directly, either with a phone call or a letter. Either way, your request should include:

- A brief rundown of your history with the creditor

- A brief explanation of the financial hardship that led to your late payment
- A request to remove the negative mark from your credit report

Of course, if you have a long history of late payments, that's another story. If you have the money, you might be able to negotiate a payment plan with them that includes paying a large lump sum amount in exchange for removing your negative marks. Calling your creditor to discuss your options, and reminds us that the removal of negative, accurate information is unlikely.

 Creditors are obligated by law and Experian policy to report accurate information about the account history. If you have a history of late payments creditors are unlikely to have those late payments removed.

"The best thing to do is to catch up on the late payments, bring the accounts current and continue to make your payments on time. The late payments will eventually be deleted in accordance with the time frames specified in the Fair Credit Reporting Act. If you are unable to do so, discuss options with your creditors. They may be able to work with you to change the account payment due date so that you are able to make the payments on time."

Beware of Debt Settlement or Consolidation

In general, pursuing debt settlement or debt consolidation is not a great idea.

Most of these companies are pretty sneaky and some of them don't even have any contact with your original creditor. Worst case scenario: you pay the company, never hear from them again, and the negative item is still on your report. If you're considering going with one of these companies, you'll want to keep a few things in mind:

Fees and sneaky, rigid contracts: Most of the time, they'll charge you a fee for settling. Worse, if you miss a payment as part of your settlement or consolidation plan, you could lose all of your money—none of it will go toward paying off your debt.

Taxes: When you settle for a lower amount, that means a portion of your past debt is forgiven. And anytime your debt is forgiven, you'll owe taxes on the amount forgiven if it's over $600.

Longer terms: You can actually pay more over time with debt consolidation. All it does is stretch out the length of your debt. Your monthly payments are smaller, but at the expense of paying more interest over time.

There's also an important distinction to be made here: debt settlement and consolidation are not the same as credit counseling. The former options, along with the credit repair industry, promise to simply erase your delinquencies–and usually at quite a cost–while the latter helps you build better habits to improve your credit over time.

"There are many excellent credit counseling services that can help you budget more effectively and who can work with your lenders to assist with debt repayment as well. Don't be afraid to ask for help," Griffin says. "Be very careful about working with any organization that promises to remove accurate but negative information from your credit report, especially if they ask for payment up front."

Credit Repair Tactics

While improving your credit score takes time, there are a few legit tips and tricks that can help you along the way.

Again, as Griffin suggests, you can catch up on missed payments by working out a hardship payment plan with your creditors. Simply give them a call and ask what programs are available. You might be surprised at their willingness to work with you–creditors would rather you pay as much as you can than nothing at all.

Also, credit utilization makes up nearly a third of your credit score, so it helps to focus on this area. In basic terms, your credit utilization is the amount of credit you have available to you versus how much of it you're actually using. The lower your credit utilization, the better.

This means if you open up a new line of credit, it should boost your score, assuming you don't actually use that credit (and after you account for the inquiry and the lowering of your average age of accounts). Problem is, when your credit isn't great, it's hard to open up new lines of credit. There are a few ways to get around it, though.

A secured credit card might be an option. These require you to deposit a large sum of money, which acts as collateral if you miss a payment.

If you have a parent or spouse with solid credit, you might consider asking them to add you as an authorized user to their credit card. Provided they haven't racked up a bunch of debt on that card, this gives you a new line of credit.

You also may want to avoid closing accounts that you've had open for a long time. Not only would this reduce your credit utilization, it also affects your credit history, which makes up a big part of your score too.

Improve Your Credit Habits

After dealing with errors and inaccuracies, you can now determine how bad your situation is and in what areas of your financial life are giving you problems. You can use the information in your credit report to see whether you have too much debt or too many outstanding bills. It can also help you realize what you need to establish good credit. If you have failed to pay a loan that your creditor had to report you to a collection agency, it will be reflected on the credit report. Knowing this information then, you can start to modify your financial habits and be quick about it. Seek out the problems and financial issues in your life that have contributed to your credit woes and use them as a guide to create an action plan that will help you to improve your credit score fast.

The bottom line is that good financial habits will help a lot in obtaining a good credit score for you. You have to accept that a low credit score somehow gives a pretty accurate picture of your financial habits, of how you deal with your debts and other financial obligations. Develop good financial habits and you will be free from debt and credit problems. Learning to budget is a good start. A budget is your own report card that tells you how much you earn and how much you can spend for the items you necessarily need. Keep this up and you will develop another good financial habit - living within your means.

You must not allow yourself to think that only more money can free you from credit problems. This is fallacious; there are people earning a lot more than you and they still have credit problems. The key is to know how to handle money and manage your debt.

STICK TO A BUDGET

Living within your means is one of the most important ways to keep your finances and your credit on track. Even if you're good at making your paychecks last each month, make sure you're tucking a portion of your money away in a savings account so that you can take care of any financial emergencies that pop up.

Tips To Help You Start Effective Personal Budgeting

• Do Not Spend More Money Than You Have- If you cannot afford to pay something in cash, it's best not to buy it-even if you have a credit card. A credit card is not free money. In fact, ideally, your credit utilization ratio should not go beyond 30 percent of your available credit to maintain a good credit score. If you go beyond 30 percent (or even worse, max out your credit card), not only will you have a difficult time paying your balances back but you will also damage your credit score. The best way to use a credit card is to use it sparingly and then pay the balance on time and in full every month.

• Avoid Adding More Debt- If you have a credit card balance or loan that is long overdue and you receive a new credit card offer in the mail, you might think that opening a new line of credit can be a good way to help you pay your older credit card balances and loans. This isn't a good idea, however, especially if you already have a poor credit score.

By adding another line of credit, you will just add more debt to your current debt, which could quickly get out of hand. Similarly, if you have a good credit score and can manage your finances responsibly, it is not a good idea to have seven or eight lines of credit. Having two or three credit cards should be sufficient and will even make tracking and paying your expenses much easier.

- Track Your Spending- Effective budgeting starts with knowing where you spend your money. Many people get their income and then wonder where their money went after only a few days. To avoid this confusion, list all of your expenses to the penny and separate your fixed expenses (the expenses you need to make every month) from your variable expenses. Examples of fixed expenses are mortgage payments, rent, electricity, water, groceries, and transportation costs, while examples of variable expenses can include trips to the coffee shop, candies bought from gasoline stations, eating out, going shopping, and other expenses that you can usually do without. The next time you receive your paycheck, before spending it, take a look at your list. The first thing you should do is to set aside the amount of money you need to pay your fixed expenses.

Then, the money left should be divided between your savings and your personal expenses. Your savings, as much as possible, should be a fixed amount. If the money left over for your personal activities is too little, take a look at your list of variable expenses and find areas where you can cut back.

• Regularly Check Your Credit History- There are people who overlook the need to check their credit reports. However, checking your credit reports is extremely important because your reports may contain errors and inaccuracies that contribute to a low credit score. By regularly checking your reports, you can have errors corrected before they do serious damage to your credit score. It is also a good idea to order your credit score every once in a while to motivate yourself to work on improving or maintaining it.

USE A SECURED CREDIT CARD RESPONSIBLY

After getting your monthly finances together, it's time to start thinking about further complementing your credit score with a credit card. If you have trouble getting approved for one, consider signing up for a secured credit card. It's specifically designed for people recovering from bad credit.

You make a security deposit in an amount that serves as your credit limit. You don't pay for your monthly balance out of that fund, it simply serves as collateral as you start to make payments on time.

The good news? By using a secured credit card, which uses money you place in a security deposit account as collateral, you can build your credit with responsible use in several meaningful ways* — as long as you follow a few rules.

1. Use for Small Purchases You Can Pay Off Each Month

The point of using a secured credit card is to show your ability to responsibly charge and then pay off your balance. To do this, make a few purchases each month and pay your bill in full and on time. By not carrying a balance, you not only avoid paying interest on purchases, but are using a time-tested strategy for building credit.

2. Pay on Time, and More Than the Minimum

While making your minimum payment on time is one essential element to a healthy credit score, upping that payment each month has added benefits. Among them: helping to pay off more of your balance, which can show that you aren't able to properly manage your money, and reducing your credit utilization ratio, or the amount you owe compared to your credit limit. Both are factors that affect your credit score.

3. Make Multiple Payments

Making more than one monthly payment can help keep your balance continually low. This is important because even if you pay in full each month, you can't be sure when your credit card issuer will send your report to the three credit agencies, and a large balance reduces your overall credit, which can negatively affect your credit score. You may also choose to send a payment after a heftier-than-normal purchase.

4. Set Payment Alerts

Even the most organized person misses a payment now and then. But when you are trying to build credit, that's one time too many. Avoid this scenario with payment alerts that remind you of your bill's upcoming due date.

You may choose to set up a "Payment Due" alert with your issuer, and be texted, or manually put together a monthly "alarm" that notifies you a week before your bill is due.

5. Enroll in Auto-Pay

Still concerned about making your payment on time? Perhaps the easiest plan is to enroll in auto-pay, which allows your issuer to automatically deduct the monthly balance from your bank account so you don't have to keep track of bills.

*: Discover reports your credit history to the three major credit bureaus so it can help build your credit if used responsibly. Late payments, delinquencies or other derogatory activity with your credit card accounts and loans may adversely impact your ability to build credit. Discover reports your credit history to the three major credit bureaus so it can help build your credit if used responsibly. Late payments, delinquencies or other derogatory activity with your credit card accounts and loans may adversely impact your ability to build credit.

CHAPTER 4

HOW TO RECOGNIZE A CREDIT REPAIR SCAM

When you're struggling with bad credit, credit repair companies sound like the perfect solution to help you get your credit back on track again. For a fee, these companies promise to remove bad information from your credit report, replace it with good information, and leave you with a much better credit score. Unfortunately, the credit repair industry is full of companies whose only goal is to scam consumers.

Being desperate for better credit can leave you vulnerable to credit repair scams. Don't let yourself be taken advantage of. Credit repair organizations are governed by a law known as the Credit Repair Organizations Act. This federal law requires any credit repair service to fulfill certain obligations to you. Any credit repair company that doesn't follow these rules is potentially a scammer.

Seven Signs Of A Credit Repair Scam You Could Be Getting Scammed If Any Of The Following Are True:

1. You aren't given a copy of the "Consumer Credit File Rights Under State and Federal Law" letting you know your rights to obtain a credit report and dispute inaccurate credit report information. All credit repair companies are required to let you know that you can perform these services on your own.

2. You aren't given a copy of the contract to view before you're asked to sign it. Do not agree or pay for services before you know what you're signing up for. Read through the contract to make sure it contains all the important information.

3. The contract doesn't contain the following information:

- The amount you are being charged
- Details about the services being performed on your behalf

- The date by which the services will be performed (or the time period required to perform the services)
- The name and business address of the organization
- A statement letting you know you can cancel the contract within 3 days

4. You're asked for payment before the services have been performed. The law prohibits credit repair companies from charging upfront fees. This is an area where many credit repair companies break the law; some companies may be unaware that they're not supposed to charge customers upfront.

5. The company promises to remove accurately reported information from your credit report. Legally, this information belongs on your credit report, but credit repair companies sometimes try shady tactics (like having you claim identity theft) to remove accurate information from your credit report.

6. The company promises to create, or asks you to create, a "new" identity with a new social security number or federal employer identification number (EIN). In one credit repair scheme, the credit repair company creates a new credit profile and you apply for all future credit products with that information instead of your old social security number.

7. You're asked to sign a form waiving your rights under the Credit Repair Organizations Act (CROA). Fortunately, the CROA voids any waiver of rights the credit repair company signs.

CAN ANY CREDIT REPAIR COMPANY BE TRUSTED?

It would be an overstatement to say that all credit repair companies are scammers. Shop around among a few different companies rather than settle on the first one you see.

Approach any company you're considering with a healthy dose of skepticism.

The credit repair company consults with you before discussing a strategy for your credit: No company can tell you exactly what they can do for your credit if they're not aware of your credit history. An honest credit repair company will ask questions about your credit history and may even view your credit reports before talking about what it will do.

The company makes sure you know your rights: You can dispute information on your own by writing to the credit bureaus, but many people would prefer to pay a company to do this work for them. That's ok. But, avoid a company who is secretive about their methods or makes it seem like they are the only ones who can repair your credit. An honest credit repair company will have a proven track record of success and can tell you why their services are better than those of other companies.

The company doesn't promise to raise your credit score a specific number of points: A credit repair company who's had success with other clients can tell you the results that previous customers have experienced, but they cannot tell you how much your credit will improve if you use their services.

If a company sounds too good to be true, there's a very good chance that it isn't true. Before you use a company's credit repair services, do some research with the Better Business Bureau (BBB), Federal Trade Commission (FTC), and your state attorney general to find out if there are any existing complaints. Avoid companies that consumers have already complained about.

AVOIDING CREDIT REPAIR SCAMS

Does it sound too good to be true? It probably is.

The Federal Trade Commission ("FTC") is cracking down on credit repair web sites that promise consumers they can restore their creditworthiness for a fee. Over 180 web sites have been put on notice that their credit repair claims may violate state and federal laws. According to the FTC, many credit repair operations "guarantee" they can remove negative information from consumers' credit report even if the negative information is accurate and timely. This is not true The FTC has also identified over 60 credit repair operations that sell instructions on how to substitute a false social security number for your current number and create a new credit identity. Doing so is a violation of federal law.

Be Aware Of False Claims:

Consumers need to remember three things about "credit repair" says Jodie Bernstein, Director of the FTC's Bureau of Consumer

Protection. "First, accurate and timely negative information cannot be removed from a credit report in an effort to repair it. Second, it's not only a bad idea to create a new credit identity using a false Social Security Number, it's also illegal.

And third, when it comes to credit repair, only time and a personal debt repayment plan will improve your credit report." If you decide to look into a credit repair offer, beware of the following warning signs offered by the FTC:

- The company wants you to pay for credit repair services before any services are provided.
- They don't tell you your legal rights and what you can do for free.
- They recommend that you not contact a credit bureau directly.

- They suggest you invent a new credit identity by applying for an Employer Identification Number to use instead of your social security number.
- They advise you to dispute all information in your credit report, or do something else that seems illegal.

Under the federal Credit Repair Organizations Act, credit repair companies can't require you to pay them until they've completed the services for which you contracted. You also have the right to cancel your contract with a credit repair company within three days of the day you sign it.

CONCLUSION

An excellent credit score and credit report can make your life much easier and much cheaper. People with excellent scores get the lowest interest rates on mortgages, the best chance of approval for loans and the cheapest auto insurance policies. Prospective employers often look at credit reports before making a hiring decision. It has never been easier to take control of your credit report and your information. Just make sure you don't fall victim to the promises of scam artists. There is no quick fix. Hopefully this guide gave you the confidence to take control of your credit report yourself. To get the best score possible, you need to fill your credit report with good information. In order to do that, make sure you:

1. Make all of your payments on time. A missed payment can have a big, negative impact on your score.
2. Have at least some activity on your credit report every month. The easiest way to do that is with a secured credit

card or a credit card. But you don't have to go into debt to get a good score. Use your card every month, but never more than 10% - 20% of the available limit. When you get your statement, make sure you pay the balance in full and on time. That way you never have to pay interest.

3. If you visit a doctor or hospital, make sure you chase for the payment information. A big portion of debt on credit reports relates to medical billing

4. issues. Don't wait for the bill. Chase your doctor and make sure you get the bill taken care of.

5. If you just keep repeated #1, #2 and #3 your score will improve over time.

If you have debt in collections now, you can read this article for tips on how to negotiate for the best settlement possible. And just remember that a bad credit score is not a life sentence. Most bad information will be off your report in 7 years, and it will become less important ever year. Anyone can get a good score with a strategy, patience and discipline.

Frequently Asked Questions

What is your credit score — and what is a good credit score?

Your credit score uses data on how you've handled debt in the past to predict your likelihood of repaying a future loan or credit card balance. The higher your score, the better you look to potential creditors. Your score affects whether you get approved for credit and sometimes the interest rate or other charges you'll pay. Check your free credit score to see where you stand.

Two companies dominate credit scoring in the U.S.: FICO and VantageScore. They calculate scores from information in your credit reports, which list your credit activity as compiled by the three major credit reporting agencies: Experian®, Equifax® and TransUnion®. If you have a good VantageScore®, you're likely to have a good FICO Score, because both consider the same factors:

Payment history: your record of on-time payments and any "derogatory" marks, such as late payments, accounts sent to collections or judgments against you.

Credit utilization: balances you owe and how much of your available credit you're using.

Age of credit history: how long you've been borrowing money.

Applications: whether you've applied for a lot of credit recently.

Type of credit: how many and what kinds of credit accounts you have, such as credit cards, installment debt (such as mortgage and car loans) or a mix. A credit score doesn't consider your income, savings or job security. That's why lenders also may consider what you owe alongside what you earn and assets you have accumulated.

Why does your credit score matter?

With a low score, you may still be able to get credit, but it will come with higher interest rates or with specific conditions, such as depositing money to get a secured credit card. You also may have to pay more for car insurance or put down deposits on utilities. Landlords might use your score to decide whether they want you as a tenant. But as you add points to your score, you'll have access to more credit products — and pay less to use them. And borrowers with scores above 750 or so have many options, including the ability to qualify for 0% financing on cars and 0% interest credit cards.

How can you build your credit score?

The two biggest factors in your score are payment history and credit utilization (how much of your available credit you're using). That's why they come first in this list of ways to boost your credit:

Pay all your bills, not just credit cards, on time. You don't want late payments or worse, a debt collection or legal judgment against you, on your credit reports.

Keep the balance on each credit card at 30% of your available credit or lower.

Keep accounts open and active if possible; that will help your length of payment history and credit utilization.

Avoid opening too many new accounts at once; new accounts lower your average account age.

Check your credit report and dispute any errors you find.

It pays to monitor your score over time. Always check the same score — otherwise, it's like trying to monitor your weight on different scales — and use the methods outlined above to build whichever score you track.

And like weight, your score may fluctuate. As long as you keep it in a healthy range, those variations won't have a major impact on your financial well-being.

What if I don't have a credit score?

If you've never had a credit card or loan, you probably won't have a score. And people who haven't used credit in years can become "credit invisible."

You are likely to have a VantageScore before you have a FICO Score. That's because VantageScore uses alternative data — such as rent or utility payments, if they're reported to the bureaus — and looks back 24 months for activity. FICO 8, the scoring model most widely used in lending decisions, looks back only six months and doesn't use alternative data.

How does NerdWallet get my score?

NerdWallet partners with TransUnion to provide your VantageScore® 3.0, based on information in your TransUnion credit report. Your score and credit report information is updated weekly.

Is my credit score really free?

Yes! You can sign in to NerdWallet at any time to see your free credit score, your free credit report information and more.

Is my information safe?

NerdWallet uses 128-bit encryption to keep your information safe. We never sell your information and you'll only be contacted by a lender if you click on a pre-qualified offer.

FICO is a registered trademark of Fair Isaac Corporation.

Thank you !

www.ingramcontent.com/pod-product-compliance
Lightning Source LLC
Chambersburg PA
CBHW070146230526
45471CB00002B/547